Password
LOGBOOK

Computer information

Internet Service Provider Name

_____

_____

Account Number :

Tech Support :

Customer Service:

Email Personal / Work :

Mail Server Type:

Incoming Server:

Outgoing Server :

Username :

Password:

Domain :

Email Personal / Work :

Mail Server Type:

Incoming Server:

Outgoing Server :

Username :

Password:

Domain :

Computer information

Internet Service Provider Name

___

___

Account Number :

Tech Support :

Customer Service:

Email Personal / Work :

Mail Server Type:

Incoming Server:

Outgoing Server :

Username :

Password:

Domain :

Email Personal / Work :

Mail Server Type:

Incoming Server:

Outgoing Server :

Username :

Password:

Domain :

Phone book

Name:
Phone:

Name:
Phone:

Name:
Phone:

Name:
Phone:

Name:
Phone:

Name:
Phone:

Name:
Phone:

Name:
Phone:

Name:
Phone:

Name:
Phone:

Name:
Phone:

Name:
Phone:

Name:
Phone:

Name:
Phone:

Name:
Phone:

Name:
Phone:

Phone book

Name:	Name:
Phone:	Phone:
Name:	Name:
Phone:	Phone:
Name:	Name:
Phone:	Phone:
Name:	Name:
Phone:	Phone:
Name:	Name:
Phone:	Phone:
Name:	Name:
Phone:	Phone:
Name:	Name:
Phone:	Phone:
Name:	Name:
Phone:	Phone:

Name:
Website:
Username :
Password :
Notes:

• •

Name:
Website:
Username :
Password :
Notes:

• •

Name:
Website:
Username :
Password :
Notes:

• •

Name:
Website:
Username :
Password :
Notes:

• •

A

Name:
Website:
Username :
Password :
Notes:

• •

Name:
Website:
Username :
Password :
Notes:

• •

Name:
Website:
Username :
Password :
Notes:

• •

Name:
Website:
Username :
Password :
Notes:

• •

Name:
Website:
Username :
Password :
Notes:

• •

Name:
Website:
Username :
Password :
Notes:

• •

Name:
Website:
Username :
Password :
Notes:

• •

Name:
Website:
Username :
Password :
Notes:

• •

A

Name:

Website:

Username :

Password :

Notes:

· ·

Name:

Website:

Username :

Password :

Notes:

· ·

Name:

Website:

Username :

Password :

Notes:

· ·

Name:

Website:

Username :

Password :

Notes:

· ·

Name:
Website:
Username :
Password :
Notes:

• •

Name:
Website:
Username :
Password :
Notes:

• •

Name:
Website:
Username :
Password :
Notes:

• •

Name:
Website:
Username :
Password :
Notes:

• •

B

Name:
Website:
Username :
Password :
Notes:

• •

Name:
Website:
Username :
Password :
Notes:

• •

Name:
Website:
Username :
Password :
Notes:

• •

Name:
Website:
Username :
Password :
Notes:

• •

Name:
Website:
Username :
Password :
Notes:

• •

Name:
Website:
Username :
Password :
Notes:

• •

Name:
Website:
Username :
Password :
Notes:

• •

Name:
Website:
Username :
Password :
Notes:

• •

B

Name:
Website:
Username :
Password :
Notes:

● ●

Name:
Website:
Username :
Password :
Notes:

● ●

Name:
Website:
Username :
Password :
Notes:

● ●

Name:
Website:
Username :
Password :
Notes:

● ●

Name:
Website:
Username :
Password :
Notes:

• •

Name:
Website:
Username :
Password :
Notes:

• •

Name:
Website:
Username :
Password :
Notes:

• •

Name:
Website:
Username :
Password :
Notes:

• •

Name:
Website:
Username :
Password :
Notes:

• •

Name:
Website:
Username :
Password :
Notes:

• •

Name:
Website:
Username :
Password :
Notes:

• •

Name:
Website:
Username :
Password :
Notes:

• •

Name:
Website:
Username :
Password :
Notes:

• •

Name:
Website:
Username :
Password :
Notes:

• •

Name:
Website:
Username :
Password :
Notes:

• •

Name:
Website:
Username :
Password :
Notes:

• •

Name: _____
Website: _____
Username : _____
Password : _____
Notes: _____
_____

· ·

Name: _____
Website: _____
Username : _____
Password : _____
Notes: _____
_____

· ·

Name: _____
Website: _____
Username : _____
Password : _____
Notes: _____
_____

· ·

Name: _____
Website: _____
Username : _____
Password : _____
Notes: _____
_____

· ·

Name:
Website:
Username :
Password :
Notes:

● ●

Name:
Website:
Username :
Password :
Notes:

● ●

Name:
Website:
Username :
Password :
Notes:

● ●

Name:
Website:
Username :
Password :
Notes:

● ●

D

Name:
Website:
Username :
Password :
Notes:

· ·

Name:
Website:
Username :
Password :
Notes:

· ·

Name:
Website:
Username :
Password :
Notes:

· ·

Name:
Website:
Username :
Password :
Notes:

· ·

Name:
Website:
Username :
Password :
Notes:

● ●

Name:
Website:
Username :
Password :
Notes:

● ●

Name:
Website:
Username :
Password :
Notes:

● ●

Name:
Website:
Username :
Password :
Notes:

● ●

D

Name:
Website:
Username :
Password :
Notes:

• •

Name:
Website:
Username :
Password :
Notes:

• •

Name:
Website:
Username :
Password :
Notes:

• •

Name:
Website:
Username :
Password :
Notes:

• •

Name:
Website:
Username :
Password :
Notes:

• •

Name:
Website:
Username :
Password :
Notes:

• •

Name:
Website:
Username :
Password :
Notes:

• •

Name:
Website:
Username :
Password :
Notes:

• •

F

Name:
Website:
Username :
Password :
Notes:

• •

Name:
Website:
Username :
Password :
Notes:

• •

Name:
Website:
Username :
Password :
Notes:

• •

Name:
Website:
Username :
Password :
Notes:

• •

Name:
Website:
Username :
Password :
Notes:

· ·

Name:
Website:
Username :
Password :
Notes:

· ·

Name:
Website:
Username :
Password :
Notes:

· ·

Name:
Website:
Username :
Password :
Notes:

· ·

F

Name:
Website:
Username :
Password :
Notes:

● ●

Name:
Website:
Username :
Password :
Notes:

● ●

Name:
Website:
Username :
Password :
Notes:

● ●

Name:
Website:
Username :
Password :
Notes:

● ●

Name:
Website:
Username :
Password :
Notes:

• •

Name:
Website:
Username :
Password :
Notes:

• •

Name:
Website:
Username :
Password :
Notes:

• •

Name:
Website:
Username :
Password :
Notes:

• •

G

Name:
Website:
Username :
Password :
Notes:

· ·

Name:
Website:
Username :
Password :
Notes:

· ·

Name:
Website:
Username :
Password :
Notes:

· ·

Name:
Website:
Username :
Password :
Notes:

· ·

Name:
Website:
Username :
Password :
Notes:

• •

Name:
Website:
Username :
Password :
Notes:

• •

Name:
Website:
Username :
Password :
Notes:

• •

Name:
Website:
Username :
Password :
Notes:

• •

G

Name:
Website:
Username :
Password :
Notes:

· ·

Name:
Website:
Username :
Password :
Notes:

· ·

Name:
Website:
Username :
Password :
Notes:

· ·

Name:
Website:
Username :
Password :
Notes:

· ·

Name:
Website:
Username :
Password :
Notes:

• •

Name:
Website:
Username :
Password :
Notes:

• •

Name:
Website:
Username :
Password :
Notes:

• •

Name:
Website:
Username :
Password :
Notes:

• •

Name: ___
Website: ___
Username : ___
Password : ___
Notes: ___
___

● ●

Name: ___
Website: ___
Username : ___
Password : ___
Notes: ___
___

● ●

Name: ___
Website: ___
Username : ___
Password : ___
Notes: ___
___

● ●

Name: ___
Website: ___
Username : ___
Password : ___
Notes: ___
___

● ●

Name:
Website:
Username :
Password :
Notes:

● ●

Name:
Website:
Username :
Password :
Notes:

● ●

Name:
Website:
Username :
Password :
Notes:

● ●

Name:
Website:
Username :
Password :
Notes:

● ●

Name:
Website:
Username :
Password :
Notes:

● ●

Name:
Website:
Username :
Password :
Notes:

● ●

Name:
Website:
Username :
Password :
Notes:

● ●

Name:
Website:
Username :
Password :
Notes:

● ●

Name:
Website:
Username :
Password :
Notes:

• •

Name:
Website:
Username :
Password :
Notes:

• •

Name:
Website:
Username :
Password :
Notes:

• •

Name:
Website:
Username :
Password :
Notes:

• •

Name:
Website:
Username :
Password :
Notes:

• •

Name:
Website:
Username :
Password :
Notes:

• •

Name:
Website:
Username :
Password :
Notes:

• •

Name:
Website:
Username :
Password :
Notes:

• •

Name:
Website:
Username :
Password :
Notes:

• •

Name:
Website:
Username :
Password :
Notes:

• •

Name:
Website:
Username :
Password :
Notes:

• •

Name:
Website:
Username :
Password :
Notes:

• •

Name:
Website:
Username :
Password :
Notes:

• •

Name:
Website:
Username :
Password :
Notes:

• •

Name:
Website:
Username :
Password :
Notes:

• •

Name:
Website:
Username :
Password :
Notes:

• •

Name:
Website:
Username :
Password :
Notes:

---

* *

Name:
Website:
Username :
Password :
Notes:

---

* *

Name:
Website:
Username :
Password :
Notes:

---

* *

Name:
Website:
Username :
Password :
Notes:

---

* *

Name:
Website:
Username :
Password :
Notes:

• •

Name:
Website:
Username :
Password :
Notes:

• •

Name:
Website:
Username :
Password :
Notes:

• •

Name:
Website:
Username :
Password :
Notes:

• •

Name:
Website:
Username :
Password :
Notes:

• •

Name:
Website:
Username :
Password :
Notes:

• •

Name:
Website:
Username :
Password :
Notes:

• •

Name:
Website:
Username :
Password :
Notes:

• •

Name:
Website:
Username :
Password :
Notes:

● ●

Name:
Website:
Username :
Password :
Notes:

● ●

Name:
Website:
Username :
Password :
Notes:

● ●

Name:
Website:
Username :
Password :
Notes:

● ●

Name: _____
Website: _____
Username : _____
Password : _____
Notes: _____
_____

● ●

Name: _____
Website: _____
Username : _____
Password : _____
Notes: _____
_____

● ●

Name: _____
Website: _____
Username : _____
Password : _____
Notes: _____
_____

● ●

Name: _____
Website: _____
Username : _____
Password : _____
Notes: _____
_____

● ●

Name:
Website:
Username :
Password :
Notes:

● ●

Name:
Website:
Username :
Password :
Notes:

● ●

Name:
Website:
Username :
Password :
Notes:

● ●

Name:
Website:
Username :
Password :
Notes:

● ●

Name:
Website:
Username :
Password :
Notes:

● ●

Name:
Website:
Username :
Password :
Notes:

● ●

Name:
Website:
Username :
Password :
Notes:

● ●

Name:
Website:
Username :
Password :
Notes:

● ●

Name:
Website:
Username :
Password :
Notes:

● ●

Name:
Website:
Username :
Password :
Notes:

● ●

Name:
Website:
Username :
Password :
Notes:

● ●

Name:
Website:
Username :
Password :
Notes:

● ●

Name:
Website:
Username :
Password :
Notes:

• •

Name:
Website:
Username :
Password :
Notes:

• •

Name:
Website:
Username :
Password :
Notes:

• •

Name:
Website:
Username :
Password :
Notes:

• •

Name:
Website:
Username :
Password :
Notes:

● ●

Name:
Website:
Username :
Password :
Notes:

● ●

Name:
Website:
Username :
Password :
Notes:

● ●

Name:
Website:
Username :
Password :
Notes:

● ●

Name:
Website:
Username :
Password :
Notes:

• •

Name:
Website:
Username :
Password :
Notes:

• •

Name:
Website:
Username :
Password :
Notes:

• •

Name:
Website:
Username :
Password :
Notes:

• •

Name:
Website:
Username :
Password :
Notes:

· ·

Name:
Website:
Username :
Password :
Notes:

· ·

Name:
Website:
Username :
Password :
Notes:

· ·

Name:
Website:
Username :
Password :
Notes:

· ·

Name:
Website:
Username :
Password :
Notes:

● ●

Name:
Website:
Username :
Password :
Notes:

● ●

Name:
Website:
Username :
Password :
Notes:

● ●

Name:
Website:
Username :
Password :
Notes:

● ●

M

Name:
Website:
Username :
Password :
Notes:

• •

Name:
Website:
Username :
Password :
Notes:

• •

Name:
Website:
Username :
Password :
Notes:

• •

Name:
Website:
Username :
Password :
Notes:

• •

Name:
Website:
Username :
Password :
Notes:

• •

Name:
Website:
Username :
Password :
Notes:

• •

Name:
Website:
Username :
Password :
Notes:

• •

Name:
Website:
Username :
Password :
Notes:

• •

M

Name:
Website:
Username :
Password :
Notes:

• •

Name:
Website:
Username :
Password :
Notes:

• •

Name:
Website:
Username :
Password :
Notes:

• •

Name:
Website:
Username :
Password :
Notes:

• •

Name:
Website:
Username :
Password :
Notes:

• •

Name:
Website:
Username :
Password :
Notes:

• •

Name:
Website:
Username :
Password :
Notes:

• •

Name:
Website:
Username :
Password :
Notes:

• •

Name:
Website:
Username :
Password :
Notes:

- - -

Name:
Website:
Username :
Password :
Notes:

- - -

Name:
Website:
Username :
Password :
Notes:

- - -

Name:
Website:
Username :
Password :
Notes:

- - -

Name:
Website:
Username :
Password :
Notes:

- -

Name:
Website:
Username :
Password :
Notes:

- -

Name:
Website:
Username :
Password :
Notes:

- -

Name:
Website:
Username :
Password :
Notes:

- -

N

Name:
Website:
Username :
Password :
Notes:

* *

Name:
Website:
Username :
Password :
Notes:

* *

Name:
Website:
Username :
Password :
Notes:

* *

Name:
Website:
Username :
Password :
Notes:

* *

Name:
Website:
Username :
Password :
Notes:

• •

Name:
Website:
Username :
Password :
Notes:

• •

Name:
Website:
Username :
Password :
Notes:

• •

Name:
Website:
Username :
Password :
Notes:

• •

Name:
Website:
Username :
Password :
Notes:

• •

Name:
Website:
Username :
Password :
Notes:

• •

Name:
Website:
Username :
Password :
Notes:

• •

Name:
Website:
Username :
Password :
Notes:

• •

Name:
Website:
Username :
Password :
Notes:

• •

Name:
Website:
Username :
Password :
Notes:

• •

Name:
Website:
Username :
Password :
Notes:

• •

Name:
Website:
Username :
Password :
Notes:

• •

Name:
Website:
Username :
Password :
Notes:

• •

Name:
Website:
Username :
Password :
Notes:

• •

Name:
Website:
Username :
Password :
Notes:

• •

Name:
Website:
Username :
Password :
Notes:

• •

Name:
Website:
Username :
Password :
Notes:

- - -

Name:
Website:
Username :
Password :
Notes:

- - -

Name:
Website:
Username :
Password :
Notes:

- - -

Name:
Website:
Username :
Password :
Notes:

- - -

P

Name: _____
Website: _____
Username : _____
Password : _____
Notes: _____
_____

● ●

Name: _____
Website: _____
Username : _____
Password : _____
Notes: _____
_____

● ●

Name: _____
Website: _____
Username : _____
Password : _____
Notes: _____
_____

● ●

Name: _____
Website: _____
Username : _____
Password : _____
Notes: _____
_____

● ●

Name:
Website:
Username :
Password :
Notes:

• •

Name:
Website:
Username :
Password :
Notes:

• •

Name:
Website:
Username :
Password :
Notes:

• •

Name:
Website:
Username :
Password :
Notes:

• •

Name:
Website:
Username :
Password :
Notes:

· ·

Name:
Website:
Username :
Password :
Notes:

· ·

Name:
Website:
Username :
Password :
Notes:

· ·

Name:
Website:
Username :
Password :
Notes:

· ·

Name:
Website:
Username :
Password :
Notes:

• •

Name:
Website:
Username :
Password :
Notes:

• •

Name:
Website:
Username :
Password :
Notes:

• •

Name:
Website:
Username :
Password :
Notes:

• •

Q

Name: _____
Website: _____
Username : _____
Password : _____
Notes: _____
_____

● ●

Name: _____
Website: _____
Username : _____
Password : _____
Notes: _____
_____

● ●

Name: _____
Website: _____
Username : _____
Password : _____
Notes: _____
_____

● ●

Name: _____
Website: _____
Username : _____
Password : _____
Notes: _____
_____

● ●

Name:
Website:
Username :
Password :
Notes:

• •

Name:
Website:
Username :
Password :
Notes:

• •

Name:
Website:
Username :
Password :
Notes:

• •

Name:
Website:
Username :
Password :
Notes:

• •

Q

Name:
Website:
Username :
Password :
Notes:

* * *

Name:
Website:
Username :
Password :
Notes:

* * *

Name:
Website:
Username :
Password :
Notes:

* * *

Name:
Website:
Username :
Password :
Notes:

* * *

Name:
Website:
Username :
Password :
Notes:

• •

Name:
Website:
Username :
Password :
Notes:

• •

Name:
Website:
Username :
Password :
Notes:

• •

Name:
Website:
Username :
Password :
Notes:

• •

R

Name:
Website:
Username :
Password :
Notes:

Name:
Website:
Username :
Password :
Notes:

Name:
Website:
Username :
Password :
Notes:

Name:
Website:
Username :
Password :
Notes:

Name:
Website:
Username :
Password :
Notes:

● ●

Name:
Website:
Username :
Password :
Notes:

● ●

Name:
Website:
Username :
Password :
Notes:

● ●

Name:
Website:
Username :
Password :
Notes:

● ●

R

Name:
_____
Website:
_____
Username :
_____
Password :
_____
Notes:
_____
_____

● ●

Name:
_____
Website:
_____
Username :
_____
Password :
_____
Notes:
_____
_____

● ●

Name:
_____
Website:
_____
Username :
_____
Password :
_____
Notes:
_____
_____

● ●

Name:
_____
Website:
_____
Username :
_____
Password :
_____
Notes:
_____
_____

● ●

Name:
Website:
Username :
Password :
Notes:

• •

Name:
Website:
Username :
Password :
Notes:

• •

Name:
Website:
Username :
Password :
Notes:

• •

Name:
Website:
Username :
Password :
Notes:

• •

S

Name: _____
Website: _____
Username : _____
Password : _____
Notes: _____
_____

• •

Name: _____
Website: _____
Username : _____
Password : _____
Notes: _____
_____

• •

Name: _____
Website: _____
Username : _____
Password : _____
Notes: _____
_____

• •

Name: _____
Website: _____
Username : _____
Password : _____
Notes: _____
_____

• •

Name:
Website:
Username :
Password :
Notes:

● ●

Name:
Website:
Username :
Password :
Notes:

● ●

Name:
Website:
Username :
Password :
Notes:

● ●

Name:
Website:
Username :
Password :
Notes:

● ●

S

Name:
Website:
Username :
Password :
Notes:

· ·

Name:
Website:
Username :
Password :
Notes:

· ·

Name:
Website:
Username :
Password :
Notes:

· ·

Name:
Website:
Username :
Password :
Notes:

· ·

Name:
Website:
Username :
Password :
Notes:

● ●

Name:
Website:
Username :
Password :
Notes:

● ●

Name:
Website:
Username :
Password :
Notes:

● ●

Name:
Website:
Username :
Password :
Notes:

● ●

Name:
Website:
Username :
Password :
Notes:

· ·

Name:
Website:
Username :
Password :
Notes:

· ·

Name:
Website:
Username :
Password :
Notes:

· ·

Name:
Website:
Username :
Password :
Notes:

· ·

Name:
Website:
Username :
Password :
Notes:

• •

Name:
Website:
Username :
Password :
Notes:

• •

Name:
Website:
Username :
Password :
Notes:

• •

Name:
Website:
Username :
Password :
Notes:

• •

T

Name: _____
Website: _____
Username : _____
Password : _____
Notes: _____
_____

• •

Name: _____
Website: _____
Username : _____
Password : _____
Notes: _____
_____

• •

Name: _____
Website: _____
Username : _____
Password : _____
Notes: _____
_____

• •

Name: _____
Website: _____
Username : _____
Password : _____
Notes: _____
_____

• •

Name:
Website:
Username :
Password :
Notes:

Name:
Website:
Username :
Password :
Notes:

Name:
Website:
Username :
Password :
Notes:

Name:
Website:
Username :
Password :
Notes:

Name:
Website:
Username :
Password :
Notes:

• •

Name:
Website:
Username :
Password :
Notes:

• •

Name:
Website:
Username :
Password :
Notes:

• •

Name:
Website:
Username :
Password :
Notes:

• •

Name:
Website:
Username :
Password :
Notes:

• •

Name:
Website:
Username :
Password :
Notes:

• •

Name:
Website:
Username :
Password :
Notes:

• •

Name:
Website:
Username :
Password :
Notes:

• •

Name:
Website:
Username :
Password :
Notes:

· ·

Name:
Website:
Username :
Password :
Notes:

· ·

Name:
Website:
Username :
Password :
Notes:

· ·

Name:
Website:
Username :
Password :
Notes:

· ·

Name:
Website:
Username :
Password :
Notes:

• •

Name:
Website:
Username :
Password :
Notes:

• •

Name:
Website:
Username :
Password :
Notes:

• •

Name:
Website:
Username :
Password :
Notes:

• •

V

Name:
Website:
Username :
Password :
Notes:

• •

Name:
Website:
Username :
Password :
Notes:

• •

Name:
Website:
Username :
Password :
Notes:

• •

Name:
Website:
Username :
Password :
Notes:

• •

Name:
Website:
Username :
Password :
Notes:

• •

Name:
Website:
Username :
Password :
Notes:

• •

Name:
Website:
Username :
Password :
Notes:

• •

Name:
Website:
Username :
Password :
Notes:

• •

Name:
Website:
Username :
Password :
Notes:

● ●

Name:
Website:
Username :
Password :
Notes:

● ●

Name:
Website:
Username :
Password :
Notes:

● ●

Name:
Website:
Username :
Password :
Notes:

● ●

Name:
Website:
Username :
Password :
Notes:

● ●

Name:
Website:
Username :
Password :
Notes:

● ●

Name:
Website:
Username :
Password :
Notes:

● ●

Name:
Website:
Username :
Password :
Notes:

● ●

Name:
Website:
Username :
Password :
Notes:

• •

Name:
Website:
Username :
Password :
Notes:

• •

Name:
Website:
Username :
Password :
Notes:

• •

Name:
Website:
Username :
Password :
Notes:

• •

Name:
Website:
Username :
Password :
Notes:

• •

Name:
Website:
Username :
Password :
Notes:

• •

Name:
Website:
Username :
Password :
Notes:

• •

Name:
Website:
Username :
Password :
Notes:

• •

Name:
Website:
Username :
Password :
Notes:

· ·

Name:
Website:
Username :
Password :
Notes:

· ·

Name:
Website:
Username :
Password :
Notes:

· ·

Name:
Website:
Username :
Password :
Notes:

· ·

Name:
Website:
Username :
Password :
Notes:

- -

Name:
Website:
Username :
Password :
Notes:

- -

Name:
Website:
Username :
Password :
Notes:

- -

Name:
Website:
Username :
Password :
Notes:

- -

Name:
Website:
Username :
Password :
Notes:

· ·

Name:
Website:
Username :
Password :
Notes:

· ·

Name:
Website:
Username :
Password :
Notes:

· ·

Name:
Website:
Username :
Password :
Notes:

· ·

Name:
Website:
Username :
Password :
Notes:

• •

Name:
Website:
Username :
Password :
Notes:

• •

Name:
Website:
Username :
Password :
Notes:

• •

Name:
Website:
Username :
Password :
Notes:

• •

Y

Name:
Website:
Username :
Password :
Notes:

● ●

Name:
Website:
Username :
Password :
Notes:

● ●

Name:
Website:
Username :
Password :
Notes:

● ●

Name:
Website:
Username :
Password :
Notes:

● ●

Name:
Website:
Username :
Password :
Notes:

• •

Name:
Website:
Username :
Password :
Notes:

• •

Name:
Website:
Username :
Password :
Notes:

• •

Name:
Website:
Username :
Password :
Notes:

• •

Z

Name: _____
Website: _____
Username : _____
Password : _____
Notes: _____
_____

• •

Name: _____
Website: _____
Username : _____
Password : _____
Notes: _____
_____

• •

Name: _____
Website: _____
Username : _____
Password : _____
Notes: _____
_____

• •

Name: _____
Website: _____
Username : _____
Password : _____
Notes: _____
_____

• •

Name:
Website:
Username :
Password :
Notes:

* *

Name:
Website:
Username :
Password :
Notes:

* *

Name:
Website:
Username :
Password :
Notes:

* *

Name:
Website:
Username :
Password :
Notes:

* *

Z

Name:
Website:
Username :
Password :
Notes:

· ·

Name:
Website:
Username :
Password :
Notes:

· ·

Name:
Website:
Username :
Password :
Notes:

· ·

Name:
Website:
Username :
Password :
Notes:

· ·

www.ingramcontent.com/pod-product-compliance
Lightning Source LLC
Chambersburg PA
CBHW070807220526
45466CB00002B/574